# ANIMAL FAMILIES

# Ants

GROLIER
EDUCATIONAL

# About this book

Why do many animals gather in family and larger groups? Why do bees dance and wolves howl? How do lions hunt together and zebras defend against them? These and hundreds of other fascinating animal behavior questions are answered in this new set of books about animal life. The books provide fascinating insights into the activities and bodies of all sorts of animals, from meerkat troop signals to honeybee nectar searches, and from ostrich feet to elephant trunks. In each book there are detailed examples of how animals behave, and how they relate to each other. Each book also has lots of photos and specially drawn illustrations. After you have read the book, if you are interested in finding out more about a particular animal, look at the Further Reading section on page 30. It has books and websites to check out. A Glossary on page 31 explains words that you may not be familiar with, and the Index on page 32 tells you where in the book to find a particular animal, behavior, or place.

Published 2001 by Grolier Educational
Sherman Turnpike
Danbury, Connecticut 06816

© 2001 Brown Partworks Limited.

Library of Congress Cataloging-in-Publication Data
Animal Families
p.cm.
Contents: v. 1. Ants/John Woodward — v. 2. Bats/John Jackson — v. 3. Bison/John Woodward — v. 4. Chimpanzees/John Woodward — v. 5. Dolphins/Bridget Giles — v. 6. Elephants/Daniel Gilpin — v. 7. Honeybees/John Woodward — v. 8. Kangaroos/Jen Green — v. 9. Lions/John Woodward — v. 10. Meerkats/Tom Jackson — v. 11. Ostriches/Jen Green — v. 12. Penguins/Daniel Gilpin — v. 13. Prairie Dogs/Jen Green — v. 14. Weaverbirds/Tim Harris — v. 15. Wolves/Jen Green — v. 16. Zebras/Bridget Giles.
ISBN 0-7172-9585-0 (set: alk. paper)
ISBN 0-7172-9586-9 (v. 1: alk. paper)
1. Animal behavior—Juvenile literature. [1. Animals—Habits and behavior.]
I. Grolier Educational Corporation.
QL751.5.A565 2001
591.5-dc21
00-042669

Printed and bound in Singapore.

FOR BROWN PARTWORKS LIMITED
*Author:* John Woodward
*Consultant:* Dr. Viccie Jenkins
*Project editor:* Tim Harris
*Managing editor:* Anne O'Daly
*Picture research:* Adrian Bentley
*Index:* Margaret Mitchell

PICTURE CREDITS
*Artworks:* AntBits Illustration
*Bruce Coleman Collection:* (Alain Compost) 8; (Christer Fredriksson) 24; (Jens Rydell) 9; (Kim Taylor) 4, 10, 12, 23, 27 above; (Luiz Claudio Marigo) 29 below; (Sir Jeremy Grayson) 15 above; (Stephen Krasemann) 21 below. *Corbis:* (Layne Kennedy) 27 below. *NHPA:* (A.N.T.) 6, 11 below; (Anthony Bannister) 15 below, 17 below, 29 above; (Daniel Heuclin) 7 below; (Dr. Ivan Polunin) 5 above; (Eric Soder) front cover, 20; (G. I. Bernard) 17 above; (Image Quest 3-D) 11 above, 18; (Martin Harvey) 21 above; (N. A. Callow) contents page, 13, 22; (R. Sorensen & J. Olsen) 28; (Stephen Dalton) title page, 19 above, 19 below; (Steve Robinson) 16; (T. Kitchin & V. Hurst) 5 below. *OSF:* (Densey Clyne/Mantis Wildlife Films) 14. *Still Pictures:* (Michel Gunther) 7 above.

Series created by Brown Partworks Limited.
Designed by Wilson Design Associates.

# Contents

# Introduction

**Ants are amazing creatures. A single ant is just a tiny insect, but since ants live in highly organized societies they can work together in teams to achieve great things.**

A column of army ants on the march can overrun a whole town, and angry swarms of stinging harvester ants can kill pigs, calves, and even children. Huge colonies of fire ants accidentally imported into the United States from South America are threatening to take over vast areas of Texas, despite a 20-year pest control program that has cost 200 million dollars! It is not surprising that the fire ants survived because ants have lived through far worse. They have been around for at least 100 million years, which means that they survived the global catastrophe that killed off the dinosaurs 65 million years ago. Since then they have spread all over Earth,

▼ *Ants are wonderful teamworkers. This wood ant carries another, which curls its body to make the load a little easier.*

*◄ These ants look like they are kissing. In fact, their mouths are touching because one is passing food to the other.*

evolving (developing over long periods of time) into 8,800 known species (types). Today, they are probably the most numerous creatures on the planet.

The success of ants really comes from one thing: their family life. Every ant colony is basically a huge family ruled over by the ant queen. All the other ants are her children, who work together to build the nest, gather food, and raise more young ants. We will see how they do this and find out what makes ants some of the most fascinating animals alive.

*▼ Highway crossing ahead. A column of African safari ants thousands strong streams across a track in Tanzania at sunrise.*

# Essential ants

Ants are vital to the way forests, grasslands, and other natural places work. In the tropical forests of South America they make up about 30 percent of the total weight of all the forest animals. Their activities are essential to the way plant foods are recycled into living plants, so if they disappeared tomorrow the forests and grasslands— and all the animals that live in them—could vanish too.

# Ant cities

**There is no such thing as a solitary ant, living a life alone. All ants live with others of their own kind in colonies that have much in common with those of honeybees.**

▲ *Sugar ant workers are busy around the colony, while winged males prepare to fly in search of queens.*

Most of the thousands of ants that live in each colony are called workers: They are females that do not breed, but, as you might expect, do most of the work. There are many different species of ants. In most species all these workers are much the same, but some—like the fearsome army ants—rear special workers with huge jaws. They act as soldiers, defending the others to the death if necessary.

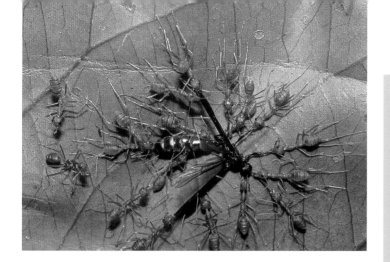

▲ *A feast to share: Workers feeding on a dead insect.*

# Programed

A queen ant produces a chemical substance called a pheromone that attracts worker ants, keeps them from breeding, and can increase the amount of foraging (searching for food) that they do. It is not known if it completely controls what the workers do, or if it simply coordinates the activity of the colony. Either way, the workers' lives are programed by their queen to some extent. And since all the workers are running the same program, they act like parts of a much bigger "superorganism" with a will of its own.

In those species of ants in which all the workers are similar, they are all likely to be called on to defend the colony in an emergency. When the crisis is over, the survivors return to other tasks. They include gathering food, building the nest, keeping it clean, feeding the young, and looking after their mother the queen. Each worker moves from one job to another until, at just a few weeks old, she wears herself out and dies.

Some ants live in very large "supercolonies" that have more than one breeding queen. At the other extreme the strange Japanese queenless ant has no queens at all, and all the workers breed instead. In a typical ant colony, though, there is just one queen. She devotes her life to laying eggs that are cared for by the workers. Most of the eggs produce replacement workers, but some become breeding females and males. They will eventually leave the nest, flying away on temporary wings (wings that do not last) to start new colonies in other places.

▼ *This queen weaver ant is tended by some of her workers.*

# Running the city

**A typical ant nest is not as spectacular as a wasp or bee nest, but it is just as complex. Instead of making paper or wax cells, the ants dig chambers and tunnels out of the earth, often building the nest into an ant hill.**

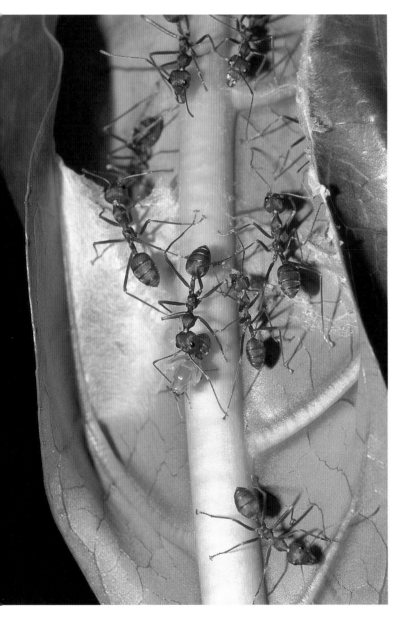

The nest of an American harvester ant, for example, may grow to well over 3 feet 3 in (1m) across and 7 in (20cm) high. It extends deep into the ground and is often surrounded by a cleared area of bare soil up to 23 feet (7m) across, with trails fanning out into the surrounding terrain.

Different ants make different styles of nest. Most dig in the earth, but carpenter ants burrow into the wood of conifer trees. Tropical weaver ants build their nests in tree foliage by fastening growing leaves together, using silk produced by their grubs (young ants). Each builder holds a grub in its jaws and uses it sort of like a tube of glue. Down on the forest floor army ants don't bother making a nest at all, but

◄ *One of the weaver ant workers is using a grub (the smaller, grayish ant) like a sewing machine to stick together two bits of leaf.*

◄ Ant nests grow bigger and bigger as the queen lays more eggs. Some ant colonies are occupied for many years and can grow above ground as well as below, producing ant hills like this.

simply link together in a living web of ants to protect their queen and her young.

The queen lives at the center of the nest, producing eggs as fast as she can. Workers carry them to incubation chambers. When the eggs hatch, the grubs (young ants) are taken to different parts of the nest. Since they are moved again when they are ready to turn into adults, there is a constant traffic of grub-carrying workers through the nest's passages. Meanwhile, the nest has to be kept clean and airy, and supplied with food. It is a real hive of industry.

► Section through a wood ant nest.

# Ant metropolis

An ant nest lasts only as long as it has a queen. But if new queens move in, it can last forever and continue growing. Sometimes many queens breed at once in the same nest. If neighboring nests link together, the ant city becomes an ant metropolis (supercity). The record is held by a single wood ant supercolony in Japan that contained over a million queens and 300 million workers in 45 connected nests.

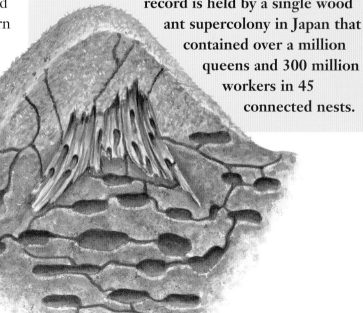

# Built for action

**An ant has the typical three-part body plan of an adult insect: a head, thorax, and abdomen. Its head carries its jaws, and in some ants special "soldiers" have extrabig jaws for fighting enemies.**

The head also carries the ant's brain and sensory organs—its eyes and antennae. Each main eye is a "compound eye" with several hundred lenses. But they do not work particularly well, and the ant relies on the acute senses of taste, scent, and touch provided by its feelers. The head is attached to the thorax by a movable neck joint. The thorax is full of muscles and carries the ant's three pairs of legs. A young queen or male also has two pairs of wings, hinged to the thorax and operated by flight muscles. After the queen's mating flight her wings fall off, and the flight muscles gradually dwindle away.

*▼ Bulldog ant workers are the largest of any ant species. They can grow up to 1¹/₂ in (3.7cm).*

At its hind end the ant's abdomen contains its digestive system, heart, and sting, if it has one: Some do, some do not.

Although an ant is built along classic insect lines, it is instantly recognizable. That is partly because of its slender waist, which has one or two extra sections linking the thorax and abdomen, rather like a string of beads. The slender waist makes its body very flexible but also vulnerable because when ants fight each other, they are often bitten in half by their rivals.

▲ *Don't mess with me! This leaf-cutter ant soldier shows off an impressive pair of jaws and its compound eyes.*

# Storage jars

In some ant species certain workers are specialized for particular jobs. Harvester ants, for example, have special food-processing workers with massive nutcracker jaws for crushing seeds. One type of wood ant has soldiers with extralarge armored heads that they use to block the nest entrances if attacked.

The weirdest, though, are the honeypot ants of America, Africa, and Australia that use young workers as living storage jars for nectar and other sweet liquid foods. The "honeypots" hang from the ceiling of the nest, and the other workers keep feeding them until their bodies swell up like balloons. When there is a drought and food is hard to find, the sugar stored in the honeypots keeps the rest of the colony alive.

◄ *Scarcely recognizable as an ant: a honeypot ant full of honeydew.*

11

# The mating game

**When an ant nest is a few years old, the queen lays batches of eggs that develop into hundreds of males and young queens. The males and the queens are bigger than the workers, and they have wings.**

The winged ants stay hidden in the nest, being fed by the workers until the big day arrives for their wedding flight. The weather has to be just right: usually a hot, damp, windless summer day. When the worker ants are sure everything is perfect, they pour out of the nest, often attacking any small animals they run into. Then they allow the winged ants to emerge. They mill around near the nest entrances for a while, then take off.

Since all the winged ants in the area take off on the same day, and even at the same time, the air is soon swarming with them. Vast numbers are eaten by birds, but some manage to pair up on the ground and mate. Each queen may mate with several males before she starts brushing them

▶ *Winged ants swarm only when conditions outside the nest are just right: hot, damp, and windless.*

# Takeover bids

Most newly mated queens start their colonies from scratch, but some have different ideas. They move into the nest of another ant species and try to kill the resident queen. Most invaders die in the attempt; but if one succeeds, the deposed queen's workers rear the new queen's eggs in a ready-made nest. As more and more eggs hatch, the new queen's workers gradually take over. Before long the whole nest has passed into new ownership.

away. The males die, their job done. But for the queen her tasks are only just beginning. She scuttles away; and since she has no more use for her wings, she breaks them off against a stone. Then she slips into a crevice to hide while her eggs mature, and she prepares to start a new colony.

► *After mating with a young queen, the winged male ant (left) will die.*

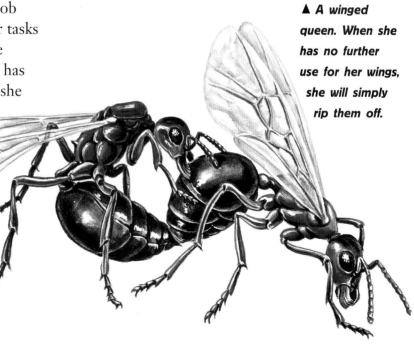

▲ *A winged queen. When she has no further use for her wings, she will simply rip them off.*

# The queen's brood

**A young queen ant may stay hidden for months after mating. She may not even eat, but survives by recycling her powerful flight muscles.**

Eventually she lays a few eggs in her refuge. When they hatch, she feeds the legless grubs with saliva enriched with reused muscle. These first grubs become tiny workers called nanitics, which start gathering food and building the nest. From then on, the queen is just an egg-laying machine.

When her next batch of eggs hatches, the grubs are better fed by the food-gathering nanitics, so they grow into full-sized workers. They are dedicated to ensuring the survival of as many new adults as possible, so the whole colony is basically an ant-making factory.

As the colony grows, so does the nest. The workers build special chambers for incubating eggs. As the grubs hatch, the workers take them to sun-warmed nurseries near the top of

▼ *Workers clamber over a queen weaver ant that has just laid a batch of eggs.*

# Egg machine

Each worker ant lives for only a few weeks, but a queen can live for 20 years or more. For most of that time she does nothing but lay eggs at a colossal rate. A fire ant queen can lay 1,500 a day, almost continuously for six years. When army ants stop marching, their queen can produce up to 300,000 eggs within 10 days! With such egg-laying power it is no wonder that ants like these form huge colonies that number millions.

▲ *Most ant eggs develop into workers, but some go on to become males and queen ants.*

the nest, helping them grow quickly. This is the part of an ant's life when it does all its growing because its maggotlike body is soft and stretchy. Within a week or so it stops feeding and becomes a pupa. During this phase its body is rebuilt into an adult ant. The adult emerges after another week to join the growing workforce.

▶ *Slender ants caring for the grubs of their colony inside a hollow branch.*

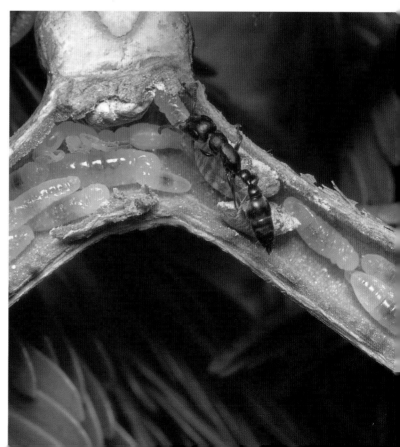

# Enemies and defenses

**Ants live in their millions all over the world, so it is not surprising that plenty of animals eat them.**

*▲ Driver ant soldiers defend their workers with massive, wickedly sharp jaws. If a few are killed, it makes no difference: They just keep coming.*

Some of them, like the anteaters of South America, are real specialists that prefer ants to any other food. Many other small mammals, birds, lizards, insects, and spiders eat them when they get the chance. So ants need to defend themselves and each other.

Some ants are so big and fierce that few animals risk tangling with them. The Australian bulldog ant, for example, grows to 1½ in (3.7cm) long and has a huge pair of jagged pincer jaws and a powerful sting in its tail. Any animal—or human—that disturbs a colony of these

# Ant wars

Some of an ant colony's worst enemies are other ants. Fire ants, for example, mount raids on other ant species, killing them and stealing their eggs and young for food. Some "slave-maker" ants even steal the pupae—young ants on the verge of becoming adults—and carry them off to their nests to hatch and work for their queen. So, any ant that meets an enemy ant while out looking for food retreats quickly to give the alarm and get reinforcements. Soon the ant armies meet and fight, and many are killed. Eventually the losers run away, and the winners take all.

▲ *Attack! Hundreds of army ants raid a leaf-cutter ant nest.*

monsters is likely to suffer a mass attack of swarming, biting, stinging ants. Yet size is not everything. The fire ants that now live in the Texas are only ⅛ in (3mm) long, but they are equally aggressive. Just walking too near their nests can drive them mad with rage, with painful results. Not all ants have stings. Wood ants spray their enemies with formic acid, and it works very well as a defense.

▶ *Size means nothing: A pugnacious ant attacks a termite soldier many times its own size.*

# Finding food

**Some ants have very fussy feeding habits, but many will eat almost anything that is worth eating. This may be nectar, cake crumbs, or even other ants. Army ants in particular forage in such large numbers that they can overwhelm giant tropical spiders. They tear them apart and carry the pieces back to their nest.**

Food-carrying is very important to worker ants. Their main concern is feeding their queen and her young, so they have to get the food to them somehow. Some workers eat on the spot and carry liquefied food back in their stomachs. They then cough it up to feed the ants and grubs in the nest. Wood ants climb trees and carry caterpillars back in their

*▼ A butterfly will make a good meal for these ants, but first it must be moved to the nest.*

# Mouth to mouth

When worker ants have food for other workers, they feed them by a process called trophallaxis. The hungry ant begs for food by tapping and stroking the other with its antennae. If it uses the right code, the provider produces a droplet of liquid food that is passed from mouth to mouth.

jaws, while harvester ants bring seeds home and give them to special seed-crackers with big jaws. They chew the seeds to a pulp, and the result is shared among the whole colony.

When one worker ant finds a good source of food, it returns to tell the others. They "talk" by rubbing their feelers together, and soon they all set off along a trail of scent left by the first scout. Some ants avoid leaving scent trails in case they attract enemies, so each ant recruits just one helper.

▲ *Ants can communicate with each other by touching their feelers.*

◀ *Different species of leaf-cutter ants collect different types of plants. This parasol ant carries a flower to its nest where it will help cultivate its fungus garden.*

# The gardeners

**Some ants move their whole colony to another place if they run out of food. Others, like the honeypot ants, store food for when times are hard. And a few kinds of ants have developed an even better solution: They grow their own food.**

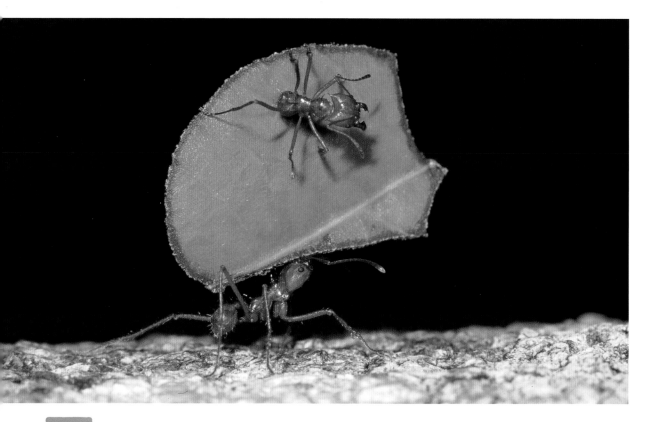

▲ *One leaf-cutter ant hitches a ride, while the other does the work!*

They are called leaf-cutter ants, and they live in the forests of tropical America. Foraging ants climb trees and scissor out sections of leaves and flower petals, then carry them back to their vast underground nests. Long columns of ants can be seen marching through the forest, with each ant carrying a piece of bright green leaf much bigger than the ant itself.

Back at the nest the ants chew the leaves to a pulp and use it as a sort of compost for growing

food—and run the risk of it running out altogether.

Each type of leaf-cutter ant grows a different type of fungus that is found only inside leaf-cutter nests. The ants keep themselves and their nests very, very clean to make sure that their gardens never grow the wrong sort of fungus—that might be poisonous to them. And when young queens leave the nest to mate and start new colonies, they have to take tiny pieces of the fungus with them to seed their own gardens.

▲ **When a supply of the right kind of leaves is found, every available ant is mustered to collect them.**

fungus. Then they use the fungus to help digest the leaves. In this way the ants are able to use a plentiful source of food (the leaves) that they would not otherwise be able to digest inside their bodies. If they did not farm the fungus, they would have to rely on less plentiful sources of

▼ **Leaf-cutter ants on a fungus garden.**

# Mutual benefit

Leaf-cutter ants could not survive without their fungus food. But it is equally true that the fungus could not survive without the ants. The ants provide the fungus with exactly the right growing conditions, keeping it moist, warm, and well fed. They do eat some of it, of course, but they cannot eat it all because they need it to keep growing. It is likely that the ants and their fungus have been living together like this for millions of years. It is an example of something called "symbiosis": an arrangement between two different types of living thing that helps them both.

# The herders

**While some ants have become gardeners, others have taken up farming. One of their favorite foods is honeydew: a sweet, sticky fluid produced by sap-sucking bugs such as aphids.**

Plant sap is mostly sugar and water, with just a little protein, so the aphids have to eat huge amounts to get the protein they need. This means they swallow too much sugar and water, and they get rid of the surplus by squirting it out their back ends as honeydew. The black garden ant and honeypot ants lap this up, since to them it is like nectar.

The ants "milk" the aphids by stroking them with their antennae to make them release the honeydew, then carry it back to the nest in their stomachs. Some ants go further than this, though. Even more amazingly, they collect aphid eggs

▼ *Red ants tending a "herd" of aphids.*

◄ *Two red ant workers helping each other with a drop of honeydew that one has collected from an aphid.*

at the end of summer and take them back to their nests. The ants look after the eggs all winter until they hatch in the spring; then they carry the young aphids out to feed.

Wherever there are big clusters of aphids on a plant, you are likely to see ants looking after them, like shepherds defending their flocks against threatening wolves.

# Farming under cover

Black garden ants have become such devoted aphid farmers that they build shelters for their herds. They collect soil grains and build them up into tubes around the stems of plants such as roses. The ants then carry their aphids into the shelters, where they can feed in safety—and be "milked" easily.

▲ *Aphids have many enemies, including ladybugs and their young, hoverfly grubs, and lacewing larvae (grubs). The ants defend the aphids against these predators—in exchange for honeydew.*

# Ant armies

**Many ants feed on plants, seeds, and sweet liquids, but a few are dedicated killers. The most ferocious of them are the army ants of tropical America and the driver ants of Africa. They are hunters that swarm through the forest in hungry hordes, thousands strong, preying on insects, spiders, centipedes, lizards, and even young birds.**

These ants are forced to keep moving by their own breeding success. An ant colony is so efficient at producing new mouths to feed that it can quickly run out of food. The problem is much worse for ants that hunt because live prey is never as plentiful as plants. Since an army ant colony can easily

▼ *A column of African driver ants on the move.*

contain a million ants—and maybe 10 times as many—they would soon strip the forest around a permanent nest. Their solution is to keep moving through the forest, killing and eating as they go, like a marauding army. An army ant column may be 3 feet (0.9m) wide and 300 feet (90m) long. This army may contain more than 600,000 individual ants. When they stop for the night, they have no time to build a true nest, so instead, the soldiers—extralarge workers with massive curved jaws—link together into a living, biting ball. Within this "bivouac" (tent) the other workers link up and form nurseries for the young and a royal chamber for their queen. Unless this is an egg-laying stop for the queen, the workers set off again at dawn, and the whole living construction melts away.

▲ *Reports of army ants devouring poisonous snakes and even tethered horses have been proven. However, stories of people being eaten alive are not thought to be true.*

# On the march

When army ants are on the march, they travel in a long column, with vulnerable workers carrying ant grubs on the inside and pincer-jawed soldiers guarding the flanks. They keep this up for about 15 days, until the grubs are ready to pupate (turn into adults). Ant pupae don't eat, so the colony can stop marching and set up camp. After five days the queen starts laying eggs. Fifteen days later all the eggs hatch at once, and all the pupae turn into new adults. Suddenly there may be up to 300,000 extra mouths to feed: Before long the raiders have looted the whole neighborhood, and they have to strike camp and go on the march again.

# The ant kingdom

**Ants are closely related to wasps and bees. They have a waist similar to that of wasps, and many species have a sting in their tail. But while all ants live in colonies with workers and queens, most wasps spend their lives as solitary hunters.**

Wasps include such creatures as the amazing tarantula hawk wasp, which stings huge hairy spiders and drags them off to its burrow to feed its young. There are also social wasps—the striped "terrorists" that always turn up at picnics. They build elaborate nests from paper and feed their grubs on chewed-up flies and caterpillars.

Bees are similar to wasps, but they do not hunt; they collect nectar and pollen instead. Many bees live solitary lives, too, but a few form societies with queens and workers. The most familiar of these are the honeybees, whose colonies are very like those of ants. They even store food as many ant species do by turning nectar into sugary, fragrant honey.

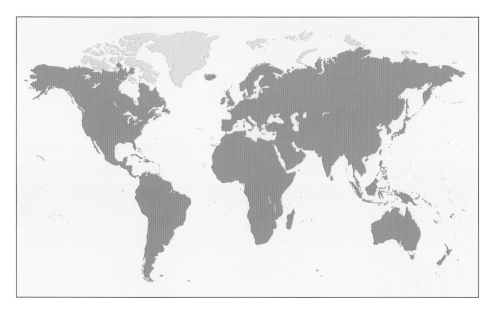

◄ **Places in the world where ants are found.**

Altogether there are at least 280,000 species of ants, wasps, and bees, grouped in about 105 families. Only about 14,000 of them are ants (with 8,800 described). They are all so similar in their way of life that they are classified in just one family: the Formicidae. Yet they range from the giant bulldog ant to tiny creatures like the ⅒ in (2mm) pharoah ant that lives in buildings and is one of the most successful insects on Earth.

◄ *A field digger wasp with a fly it has captured to eat.*

# Ancestral ants

Ants are very sophisticated insects that have been evolving (developing) over a very long time. The oldest known ant was found preserved in a lump of amber, or fossilized tree resin. The amber formed in the mid-Cretaceous period, 100 million years ago—30 million years before the appearance of the ferocious dinosaur *Tyrannosaurus rex*. So ants have been around for about 1,000 times longer than humans have. It is likely that when all the people have vanished from Earth, the ants will still be here.

► *Perfectly preserved in amber, this winged ant lived about 35 million years ago.*

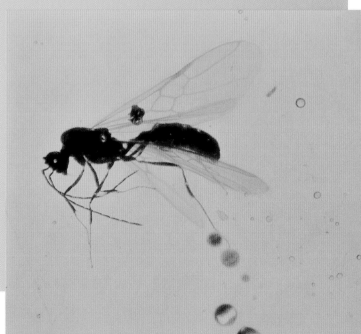

# Ants and people

**Most people do not like ants. They see them as a nuisance, and in some countries they have good reason.**

The big black carpenter ants of North America nest in wood. If they decide to move into a wooden house, they can eat away so much timber that the house collapses. The tiny pharoah ants that live in centrally heated buildings can carry infections; so when they get into hospitals, they can be a real health problem.

Mostly, though, ants are a nuisance because they bite, sting, or both. The fire ants of Texas are notorious for this. Since they now live in extremely large supercolonies, they can turn whole fields into no-go areas. In the tropics people live in dread of marching army ants that attack anything in their path. In 1973 a huge colony was reported to have plundered the town of Goiandira in Brazil and eaten its chief of police before being driven away by people with flamethrowers.

Yet even army ants are not all bad. When they pass close to a village, they clear the area of insect pests. In 1968 there was a

▼ *This old wooden building has been eaten by ants.*

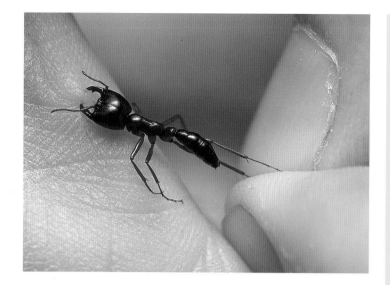

# Ant conservation

Nobody knows quite how many species of ants there are. Yet most scientists believe there are thousands of undiscovered species in the tropical forests. Since these forests are being destroyed very quickly, many of these species will probably disappear before we get a chance to find them. Does this matter? The truth is that we do not know. What we do know is that ants are an important part of the web of life on Earth. If parts of this web are destroyed, then eventually it will collapse.

famine in Biafra, Nigeria, and starving people were able to keep their children alive by feeding them on huge winged male driver ants called "sausage flies." In Australia the native tribespeople use the honey from swollen honeypot ants for food and medicine. And most ants, of course, are really no trouble at all.

▲ *Ouch! A driver ant biting a human hand.*

▼ *The biggest threat to ants—like so many other animals—comes from the clearing of rain forests.*

# Further reading

**Ant**
by Michael Chinnery (Troll Associates, 1991).

**Ants**
by Ruth Berman (Lerner Publications, 1996).

**Ants**
by Christine Butterworth (Silver Burdett Press, 1988).

**Ants**
by Cheryl Coughlan (Pebble Books, 1999).

**Ants**
by Eileen Everett (Rourke, 1981).

**Ant Cities**
by Arthur Dorros (Crowell, 1987).

**Garden Wildlife: The Living World of Your Garden**
by Derek Jones (Ebury, 1981)

**How Insects Work Together**
by Jill Bailey (Benchmark Books, 1998).

**How Many Ants?**
by Larry Dane Brimmer (Children's Press, 1997).

**Insects and Spiders**
by Penny Clarke (Franklin Watts, 1995).

**Ways of the Ant**
by John Crompton (Lyons, 1988).

## Web sites

www.earthlife.net
www.entsoc.org
www.ex.ac.uk/bugclub
www.theaes.org

## Useful addresses

**Amateur Entomologists' Society**
P. O. Box 8774
London SW7 5ZG.
www.theaes.org

**Entomological Society of America**
9301 Annapolis Road, Lanham, MD 20706.
www.entsoc.org

**Worldwide Fund for Nature**
1250 24th Street NW, Washington, DC 20037.
www.panda.org

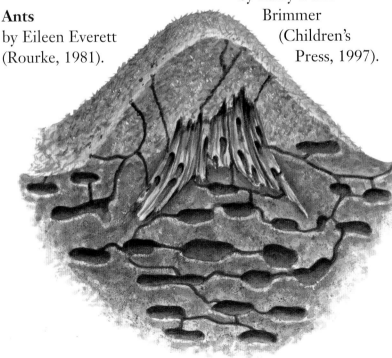

# Glossary

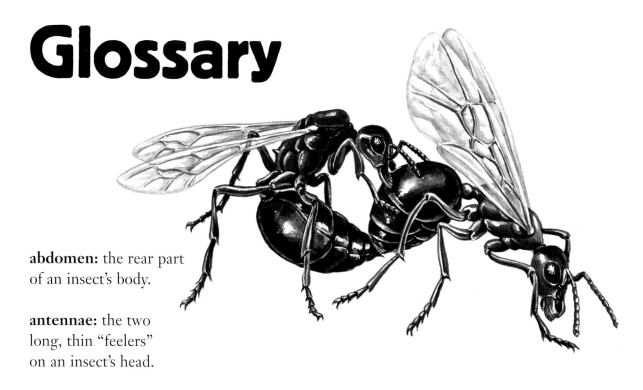

**abdomen:** the rear part of an insect's body.

**antennae:** the two long, thin "feelers" on an insect's head.

**evolve:** when an animal species changes very slowly so that the animals are better suited to the conditions in which they live.

**forage:** go in search of food.

**larvae:** insect grubs.

**nanitics:** the first worker ants to be produced in a new colony.

**nectar:** the water and sugar mixture that is found in flowers. Bees feed on this to get energy.

**pollen:** the protein powder that bees feed on. It is important for their growth. The movement of pollen from one flower to another also fertilizes plants and enables the growth of seeds and fruits.

**pupa:** the stage in an ant's life between the grub (or larva) and the adult form.

**regurgitate:** when an adult ant coughs up partially digested food to feed others in the colony.

**saliva:** liquid produced by an ant through its mouth to feed its grubs.

**superorganism:** many animals acting together as one. An ant colony behaves this way.

**thorax:** the middle section of an insect's body. The thorax supports its legs and (if it has them) its wings.

**trophallaxis:** when ants pass food to each other from mouth to mouth.

# Index